An I Can Read Book™

The Bug in Teacher's Coffee

and Other School Poems

by Kalli Dakos
pictures by Mike Reed

HarperCollins*Publishers*

HarperCollins®, 📖®, and I Can Read Book®
are registered trademarks of HarperCollins Publishers Inc.

The Bug in Teacher's Coffee
And Other School Poems
Text copyright © 1999 by Kalli Dakos
Illustrations copyright © 1999 by Mike Reed
Printed in the U.S.A. All rights reserved.

Library of Congress Cataloging-in-Publication Data
Dakos, Kalli.
    The bug in teacher's coffee / Kalli Dakos ; pictures by Mike Reed.
        p.   cm. — (An I can read book)
    Summary: A collection of simple poems depict the activities at school from the morning
welcome until the closing bell.
    ISBN 0-06-027940-0 (lib. bdg.).— ISBN 0-06-027939-7
    1. Education, Elementary—Juvenile poetry.   2. Elementary schools—Juvenile poetry.
3. Children's poetry, American.   [1. Schools—Poetry.   2. American poetry.]   I. Reed, Mike,
1951–   ill.   II. Title.   III. Series.
PS3554.A414B8   1999   98-54209
811'.54—dc21   CIP
                                                                                                  AC

1   2   3   4   5   6   7   8   9   10
❖
First Edition

http://www.harperchildrens.com

For my cousin, Peter,
and his wife, Lois
(Mrs. Copis to her students),
and for all the stories
we've shared through the years.
—K.D.

To Joe and Alex
—M.R.

Contents

Good Morning

My hallways are clean,

My classrooms are too,

Good morning,

Good morning,

I'm ready for you.

My windows are shining,

This day is brand new,

Good morning,

Good morning,

I'm waiting for you.

Front Door

Keep me shut,

I have the flu,

Achooooooooo!

            Achooooooooo!

Achooooooooo!

            Achooooooooo!

Keep me shut,

I have the flu.

The Class Goldfish (1)

Around and around and around I go,

Sometimes *fast*,

Sometimes s l o w,

Around and around and around I go.

Math Test

One plus one is NOT three.

Three plus three is NOT four.

My owner needs to study more.

Bee

I'll scare the kids in room one.

Buzzzzzzzzzzzzzzzzzzzzzzzzzzzz.

I'll scare the kids in room two.

Buzzzzzzzzzzzzzzzzzzzzzzzzzzz.

I'll scare the kids in room three.

Buzzzzzzzzzzzzzzzzzzzzzzzzzz.

I'll scare the kids in room four.

Buzzzzzzzzzzzzzzzzzzzzzzzzzzz.

I'll scare the kids in room five!

Buzzzzzz———HELP!

Someone's after me!

I'm buzzing back to the hive.

13

Jack's Pencil

I've been taken hostage

By that creepy kid, Clark.

He stuck me in his desk,

Where it's smelly and dark.

He won't let me out,

And he won't give me back.

I'm sitting here yelling,

"I'm in the desk,
Jaaaaaaaaaaaaaaack!"

Happy Birthday to You

Book: Happy birthday to you,

Happy birthday to you,

Happy birthday dear ruler,

Happy birthday to you.

Ruler: It's not my birthday.

Book: Happy unbirthday to you,

Happy unbirthday to you,

Happy unbirthday dear ruler,

Happy unbirthday to you.

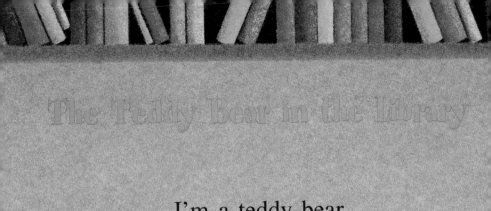

I'm a teddy bear

You can tell anything to.

I'll never peep,

Or tell on you.

18

Comb

Where's my owner?

Does anyone know?

She lost me yesterday,

Where did she go?

Is THAT her?

Oh noooooooooooooo!

Flying Around the Classroom

Fly 1:   A kid in here

Eats flies.

Pass it on.

Fly 2:   Oh my!

A kid in here

Eats flies.

Pass it on.

Fly 3:   Oh my!

         A kid in here

         Eats flies.

         Pass it on.

Fly 4:   Oh my!

         A kid in here

         Eats flies.

         Pass it . . .

         GULP!

         I'm gone!

Gym

My head is aching,

Bong!

Bong!

Bong!

The balls are bouncing

All day long.

I'm trying so hard

To be strong.

My head is aching,

Bong!

Bong!

Bong!

23

Monkey Bars

Rightside up,

And upside down,

Back and forth,

And all around,

The kids

Are making monkey sounds!

Slide

Wheeeeeeeeeeeee!

Wheeeeeeeeeeeeeee!

Children love to slide

down

me!

David Grabs Me

David grabs me

And he

runs

    runs

        runs

            runs

                runs

                    runs

                        runs

                    runs

                  runs

                  Yeah!

                  A score!

The Class Goldfish (2)

Around and around and around I go,

Today I'm swimming

To Mexico,

Around and around and around I go.

Cold Dog on a Tray

I've been waiting
So long on this tray,
I'm not a hot dog,
I'm a COLD dog today.

The Bug in Teacher's Coffee

It's warm,

It's warm,

I'll climb right in,

I'm going for

A little swim.

It's fun,

It's fun,

I want to stay,

Where I can swim,

And swim all day.

OH NO!

Ahhhhhhhhhhhhhhhhhhhh!

Mr. Robins!

Schools Get Hungry Too

I'd like a bowl

Of ruler stew,

A pencil sandwich,

And some glue.

Some purple paint,

I'd like to drink,

And for dessert,

A classroom sink.

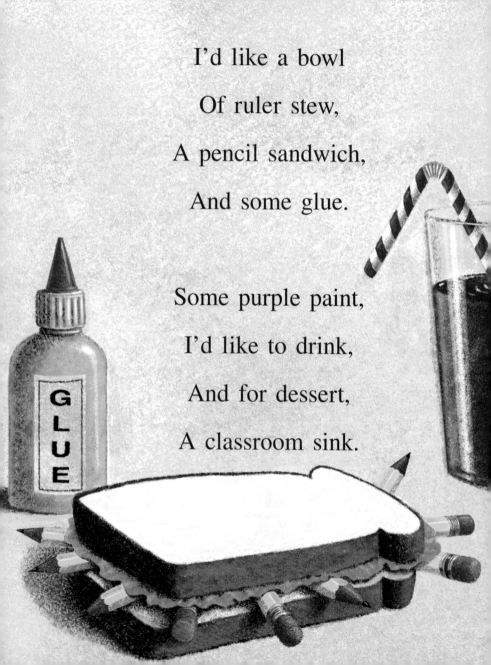

I'm the Teacher's Cookie

I'm the teacher's cookie,

I'm as GORGEOUS

As can be.

I'm the teacher's cookie,

So

Ten Ants in the Classroom

Ten ants

Looking for a treat,

Find a cake,

And it tastes sweet.

They tell their friends.

Twenty ants

Looking for a treat,

Find a juice box,

And it tastes sweet.

They tell their friends.

Thirty ants

Looking for a treat,

Find a lollipop

And it tastes sweet.

They tell their friends.

Forty ants

Looking for a treat,

Find a chocolate bar

And it tastes sweet.

They tell their friends.

35

Fifty ants

Looking for a treat,

Find a teacher

Who isn't sweet.

And she sprays them!

*They **don't** tell their friends!*

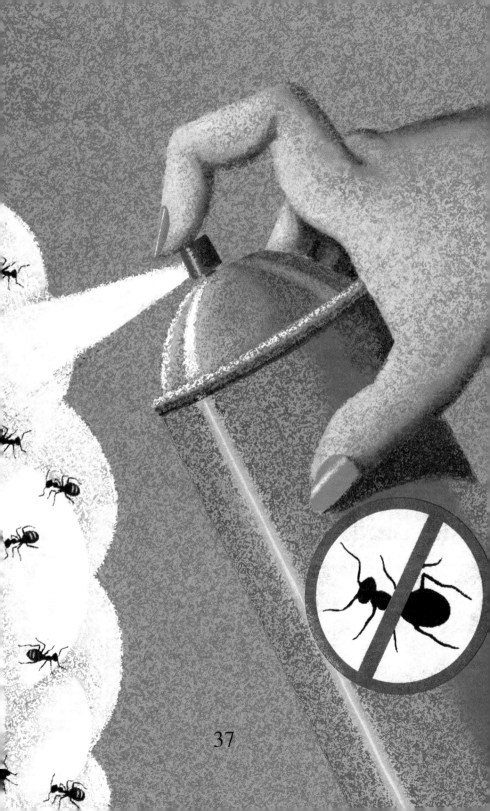

Snowflake Peeking in the Window

It would be super cool,

If snowflakes went to school.

The Class Goldfish (3)

Around and around and around I go,

I wish I could

Play in the snow,

Around and around and around I go.

The School Bell

At the end of the day,

I start to sing,

Five seconds,

Four seconds,

Three seconds,

Two seconds,

One second,

Then I

r r r r r r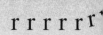